3

Super Structures

Fiona Undrill

## Contents

D1445848

**OXFORD**

UNIVERSITY PRESS

# OXFORD
## UNIVERSITY PRESS

Great Clarendon Street, Oxford OX2 6DP

Oxford University Press is a department of the University of Oxford. It furthers the University's objective of excellence in research, scholarship, and education by publishing worldwide in

Oxford  New York

Auckland  Cape Town  Dar es Salaam  Hong Kong  Karachi
Kuala Lumpur  Madrid  Melbourne  Mexico City  Nairobi
New Delhi  Shanghai  Taipei  Toronto

With offices in

Argentina  Austria  Brazil  Chile  Czech Republic  France
Greece  Guatemala  Hungary  Italy  Japan  Poland  Portugal
Singapore  South Korea  Switzerland  Thailand  Turkey
Ukraine  Vietnam

OXFORD and OXFORD ENGLISH are registered trade marks
of Oxford University Press in the UK and in certain other
countries

First published 2010
2014  2013  2012  2011  2010
10  9  8  7  6  5  4  3  2  1

ISBN: 978 0 19 464381 8

An Audio CD Pack containing this book and a CD is also available
ISBN: 978 019 464421 1
The CD has a choice of American and British English
recordings of the complete text.

An accompanying Activity Book is also available,
ISBN: 978 019 464391 7

Printed in China

ACKNOWLEDGEMENTS
*Illustrations by*: Rebecca Halls/The Organisation pp 4, 6, 7, 8, 20, 25, 26, 28, 30; Alan Rowe pp 36, 41, 45, 46, 47; Gary Swift pp 5, 15, 19

*The Publishers would also like to thank the following for their kind permission to reproduce photographs and other copyright material*: Alamy pp 5, 10, 14, 17, 22, 23 (wombat), 34; Corbis pp 8, 23 (beaver/dam), 32 (Beijing airport); Dr David Fisher, Dynamic Architecture, All rights reserved p 15; Getty Images p 9; NASA Images p 20, 21; Oxford University Press pp 3, 6, 13, 16, 32 (Beijing Stadium); Poseidon Undersea Resorts, LLC p 18; Rex Features p 12; TopFoto pp 4, 7; SuperStock p 11; www.7-t.co.uk/British Antarctic Survey p 19.

 # Introduction

A structure is something made with many parts, like a house, a school, or a bridge. It can be made of different materials like bricks, concrete, glass, wood, or metal. A super structure is very big, very long, or very tall.

What structures can you see here?
How many parts can you see?
What are the structures made of?
What other structures can you think of?

Discover!
Now read and discover more about super structures!

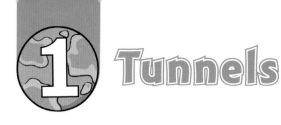

# Tunnels

Tunnels go underwater, underground, or through the ground. We use tunnels for mines, trains, and road traffic, or to carry things like gas or water. Tunnels are usually made of metal and concrete.

One of the longest tunnels in the world is the Seikan Tunnel in Japan. It's nearly 54 kilometers long! It goes between two islands. It was built because it's too dangerous to travel by boat. The tunnel is for trains, but now many people prefer to travel by plane.

Seikan Tunnel, Japan

tunnel

One of the longest road tunnels is the Laerdal Tunnel in Norway. The tunnel is nearly 25 kilometers long and it goes through a mountain. It was built because there's too much snow on the mountain roads in winter.

Laerdal Tunnel, Norway

Discover!

In the tunnel there are three big caves where drivers can stop and rest.

Go to pages 24–25 for activities.

# Bridges

Bridges go over water or overground.

On a beam bridge, the pillars carry the deck. One of the longest beam bridges is the Lake Pontchartrain Causeway in the USA. This bridge is about 38 kilometers long and it has over 9,000 concrete pillars. It goes over water and carries road traffic.

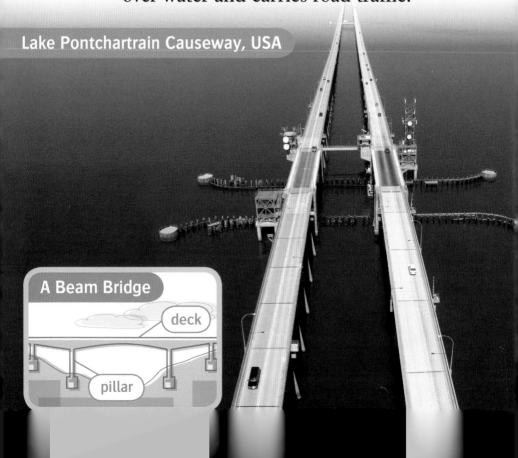

Lake Pontchartrain Causeway, USA

**A Beam Bridge**

deck

pillar

On a suspension bridge, the cables and towers carry the deck. The anchorages hold the cables.

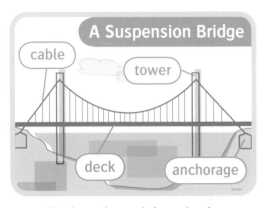

A Suspension Bridge

cable

tower

deck

anchorage

Suspension bridges move a little when it's windy. This isn't usually a problem, but in 1940 the Tacoma Bridge in the USA collapsed in light winds. It was only four months old.

Tacoma Bridge, USA

Go to pages 26–27 for activities.

# 3 Skyscrapers

Petronas Twin Towers, Malaysia

When there isn't much ground, we can build tall buildings. Very tall buildings are called skyscrapers. The first skyscraper was the Home Insurance Building. It was built in Chicago in the USA in 1885. It was 42 meters tall. The tallest skyscrapers are now much taller than this.

The Petronas Twin Towers in Kuala Lumpur in Malaysia are the tallest twin buildings. There is a bridge between the two towers called a skybridge.

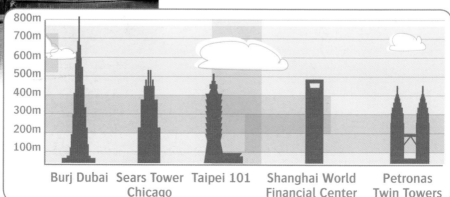

| | | | | | |
|---|---|---|---|---|---|
| 800m | | | | | |
| 700m | | | | | |
| 600m | | | | | |
| 500m | | | | | |
| 400m | | | | | |
| 300m | | | | | |
| 200m | | | | | |
| 100m | | | | | |

Burj Dubai | Sears Tower Chicago | Taipei 101 | Shanghai World Financial Center | Petronas Twin Towers

One of the tallest skyscrapers is the Burj Dubai. It's in Dubai in the United Arab Emirates. It's 818 meters tall – that's nearly a kilometer! It's made of a special, strong concrete called reinforced concrete. The Burj Dubai has apartments, shops, swimming pools, hotels, restaurants, and a library. It's like a very tall town! Do you like it?

**Discover!**

The concrete in the Burj Dubai weighs the same as about 100,000 elephants!

Burj Dubai, United Arab Emirates

Go to pages 28–29 for activities.

# Dams

Some of the biggest structures are dams. They hold back water and make a lake called a reservoir. Dams supply water, stop floods, and they also make electricity.

Gravity dams are made of a lot of concrete. They are very big and heavy, and this weight holds back the water. The Itaipu Dam is a gravity dam. It's in South America between Paraguay and Brazil. It's 196 meters tall and nearly 8 kilometers long.

Itaipu Dam, South America

Arch dams are also made of concrete. They are usually smaller than gravity dams and they are curved. The curve holds back the water. The Moiry Dam in Switzerland is an arch dam. It's 148 meters tall and 610 meters long.

Moiry Dam, Switzerland

Discover!

The first dam was built more than 4,000 years ago in Egypt. It never worked because it fell down in heavy rain.

Go to pages 30–31 for activities.

# 5 Olympic Structures

There are many super structures in Beijing in China. Some of them were built for the Olympics in 2008.

Terminal 3 of Beijing Capital International Airport is one of the biggest airport terminals in the world. The floor area is more than a square kilometer. There are seven floors, and two of the floors are underground.

**Beijing Capital International Airport, China**

**Discover!** Red and gold are traditional colors for Chinese buildings. Red is the Chinese color for good luck.

The Beijing National Stadium is one of the biggest metal buildings. It's red and gold. It has 80,000 seats. There were 11,000 extra seats for the Olympics. It also has underground pipes to make it warm in winter and cool in summer.

Sometimes it's called the Bird's Nest – can you see why?

Go to pages 32–33 for activities.

13

# Different Shapes

With new building materials, people can build structures in many different shapes.

The O2, in London in the United Kingdom, is a dome. It was built for the millennium, the year 2000. The roof is made of a special plastic and glass material. It's 365 meters wide – one meter for every day of the year. It has also 12 support towers – one tower for every month of the year.

**O2, United Kingdom**

In 2008, David Fisher designed the first rotating skyscraper. It uses energy from the wind. People want to build these rotating skyscrapers in Dubai and in Moscow.

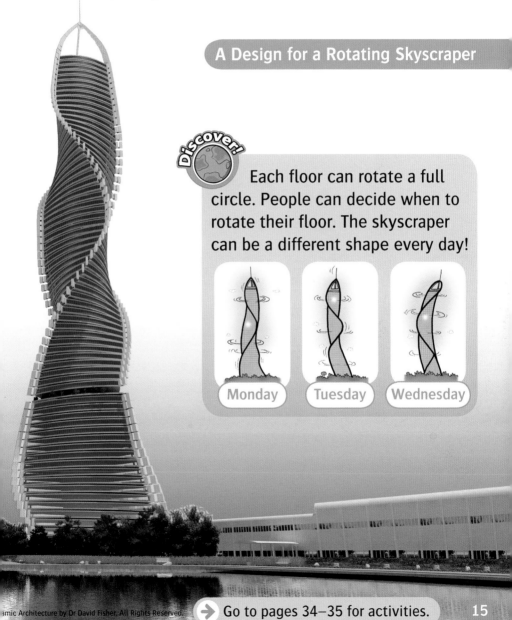

A Design for a Rotating Skyscraper

Discover!

Each floor can rotate a full circle. People can decide when to rotate their floor. The skyscraper can be a different shape every day!

Monday   Tuesday   Wednesday

Go to pages 34–35 for activities.

# 7 Glass and Ice

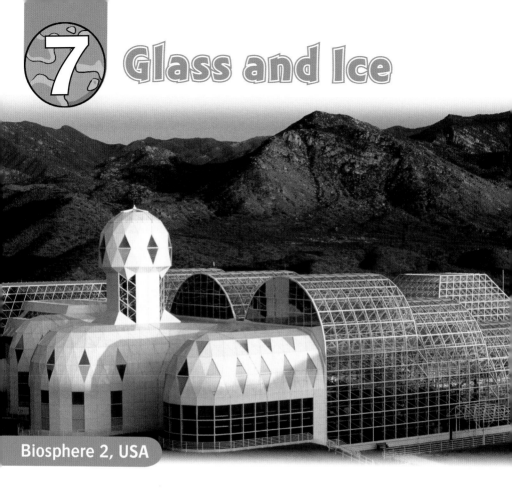

Biosphere 2, USA

Most buildings are made of concrete, bricks, metal, or wood. Some buildings use different materials.

Biosphere 2 in Arizona in the USA is made of glass and metal. It's nearly as big as two and a half American football fields. Inside, there's a rainforest, an ocean, a desert, a farm, and places for people to live and work. It's a research center.

In a village in Sweden, near the Arctic, there is a hotel made of ice called Ice Hotel. The hotel is open from December to April. It has 80 rooms. There are ice sculptures in the rooms. The beds, chairs, and tables are also made of ice. Even the drinking glasses are made of ice!

Ice Hotel, Sweden

**Discover!** Every year, Ice Hotel is built again with new ice.

Go to pages 36–37 for activities.

Did you know that people also build structures under the ocean and on ice?

The Poseidon Undersea Resort in Fiji is a hotel 12 meters under the ocean. It's made of very strong metal and plastic. The windows are made of special, clear plastic, so people can see fish and other ocean animals from the hotel. To get to the hotel, you travel by submarine!

**Poseidon Undersea Resort, Fiji**

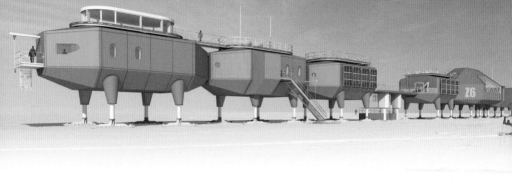

Halley 6 is a research station in the Antarctic. It's built on ice. The ice moves 400 meters every year and the structure moves with it. Halley 6 is on skis so people can move it back to the right place. Building in the Antarctic is very difficult because of the very, very cold weather.

**Discover!**

In the Antarctic, the wind speed can be 150 kilometers per hour. The temperature can be less than –50 degrees centigrade.

Go to pages 38–39 for activities.

# Structures in Space

There are also structures in space. The International Space Station (ISS) is a research station. It's about 350 kilometers above Earth.

It goes around Earth about 16 times every day. It travels at 27,700 kilometers per hour – that's nearly 8 kilometers per second!

International Space Station

You can see the ISS from Earth without a telescope.

The ISS is made of metal. It uses energy from the sun. The first part of the ISS went into space in a rocket in 1998. No astronauts went with it. Most other parts went with astronauts. Sometimes, astronauts do a spacewalk outside the ISS to attach new parts.

**An Astronaut Doing a Spacewalk**

Go to pages 40–41 for activities.

# Animal Structures

Animals can build super structures, too!

Termites build their homes with mud. These homes are tall towers called termite mounds. The tallest termite mounds are about 13 meters high. They are termite skyscrapers!

**Termite Mounds**

Discover!

Termites are insects. The tallest termite mounds are thousands of termites tall!

Wombats build underground tunnels called burrows. They dig with their front paws and bite through things with their teeth. A wombat can dig about 2 meters per hour.

Beavers build dams on the water to protect themselves from other wild animals like bears. They build the dams with small trees, stones, and mud. Their dams can be a kilometer long.

A Beaver Dam

Go to activities on pages 42–43.

# ① Tunnels

← Read pages 4–5.

## 1  Match.

1  It was built because there's too much snow on the mountain roads in winter.

2  It was built because it's too dangerous to travel by boat.

3  It's for road traffic.

4  It's for trains.

Seikan Tunnel

Laerdal Tunnel

## 2  Write *true* or *false*.

1  Tunnels can carry water.  _true_

2  The Seikan Tunnel is longer than the Laerdal Tunnel.  _____

3  The Laerdal Tunnel is shorter than the Seikan Tunnel.  _____

4  The Seikan Tunnel goes through water.  _____

5  It's quicker to use the Seikan Tunnel than to travel by plane.  _____

**3** Circle the correct words.

1 Tunnels go (under) / **over** water or ground.

2 Tunnels are made of metal and **glass** / **concrete**.

3 The Seikan Tunnel is in **China** / **Japan**.

4 The Laerdal Tunnel is in **Spain** / **Norway**.

**4** Complete the sentences.

through   longest   ~~metal~~   25 kilometers   under

1 Tunnels are usually made of _metal_ and concrete.

2 The Seikan Tunnel is one of the _____ tunnels.

3 The Laerdal Tunnel is nearly _____ long.

4 The Seikan Tunnel goes _____ the water.

5 The Laerdal Tunnel goes _____ a mountain.

**5** Write *A* or *B*.

1 Which is the longest tunnel? _A_

2 Which tunnel goes underground? ____

3 Which tunnel is for trains? ____

4 Which is the shortest tunnel? ____

5 Which tunnel goes underwater? ____

6 Which tunnel is for cars? ____

# ② Bridges

← Read pages 6–7.

## 1 Circle the correct words.

1 Bridges go **underground** / **overground**.

2 The **longest** / **shortest** beam bridge is in the USA.

3 Beam bridges and suspension bridges both have a **tower** / **deck**.

4 The Tacoma Bridge is a **beam** / **suspension** bridge.

## 2 Write the words.

> cable   deck   pillar   deck   anchorage
> tower   suspension bridge   ~~beam bridge~~

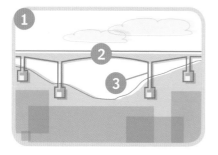 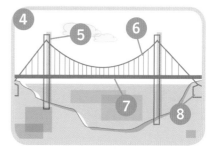

1  _beam bridge_            5  _____

2  _____             6  _____

3  _____             7  _____

4  _____             8  _____

## 3 Find and write the words.

| g | h | b | b | r | i | d | g | e | w |
|---|---|---|---|---|---|---|---|---|---|
| a | n | c | h | o | r | a | g | e | t |
| h | z | b | e | j | c | e | w | g | o |
| b | a | e | d | o | a | r | a | m | w |
| e | s | a | e | l | b | t | t | h | e |
| a | n | t | c | w | l | b | e | q | r |
| m | e | l | k | a | e | r | r | u | i |
| o | f | e | i | h | r | i | o | a | c |
| p | a | v | s | n | g | d | m | t | e |
| p | i | l | l | a | r | c | n | o | a |

1 b r i d g e
2 w _ _ _ _
3 b _ _ _
4 c _ _ _ _
5 d _ _ _
6 p _ _ _ _ _
7 t _ _ _ _
8 a _ _ _ _ _ _ _ _

## 4 Answer the questions.

1 What carries the deck on a beam bridge?

   The pillars carry the deck.

2 What carries the deck on a suspension bridge?

   _____

3 What is a problem for suspension bridges?

   _____

4 Which bridge collapsed when it was windy?

   _____

5 Write about a bridge in your country.

   _____

   _____

# ③ Skyscrapers

← Read pages 8–9.

## 1  Match.

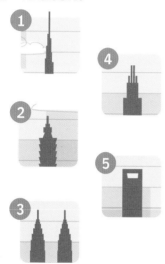

Sears Tower

Petronas Twin Towers

Taipei 101

Shanghai World
Financial Center

Burj Dubai

## 2  Write the numbers.

> 10mm   900m   1,000m   92cm   100cm   ~~8mm~~

1  about a centimeter  _8mm_

2  about a meter _____

3  about a kilometer _____

4  the same as a centimeter _____

5  the same as a meter _____

6  the same as a kilometer _____

## 3 Complete the sentences.

1 The Taipei 101 is _shorter_ than the Sears Tower.
(short / shorter / shortest)

2 The Shanghai Financial Center is _____ than
the Petronas Twin Towers. (tall / taller / tallest)

3 The Burj Dubai is the _____ skyscraper.
(tall / taller / tallest)

4 The Sears Tower is _____ than the Taipei 101.
(tall / taller / tallest)

5 The Sears Tower is _____ than the Burj Dubai.
(short / shorter / shortest)

## 4 Answer the questions.

1 Where was the world's first skyscraper built?

_____

2 How tall is the Burj Dubai?

_____

3 What are the tallest twin buildings called?

_____

4 What is your favorite skyscraper? Why?

_____

_____

_____

# 4 Dams

← Read pages 10–11.

**1 Write the words.**

reservoir   curve   arch dam
concrete   gravity dam   reservoir

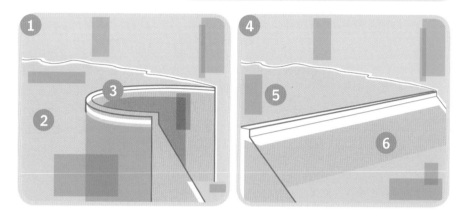

1 _____      4 _____

2 _____      5 _____

3 _____      6 _____

**2 Write *true* or *false*.**

1 Dams make water. _____

2 A reservoir is like a lake. _____

3 Dams supply food. _____

4 Dams stop floods. _____

5 The Itaipu Dam is taller than
  the Moiry Dam. _____

## 3 Complete the puzzle.

1 The first dam built fell down in heavy ___.
2 The Moiry Dam is in ___.
3 Gravity dams are very ___.
4 Gravity dams are made of a lot of ___.
5 Arch dams are ___.
6 Dams hold back ___.

*(Crossword grid with letters r, a, i, n visible reading down from clue 1)*

## 4 Answer the questions.

1 What type of dam is the Itaipu Dam?

_____

2 Where is the Moiry Dam?

_____

3 With an arch dam, what holds back the water?

_____

4 With a gravity dam, what holds back the water?

_____

5 Write about a dam in your country.

_____

_____

# 5 Olympic Structures

← Read pages 12–13.

## 1 Match.

1 It's made of metal.

2 The floor area is more than a square kilometer.

3 It has 80,000 seats.

4 Sometimes it's called the Bird's Nest.

5 It's one of the biggest airport terminals.

National Stadium

Terminal 3

## 2 Circle the correct words.

1 Terminal 3, Beijing Capital International Airport:

It's in **Russia** / **China** / **the USA**.

It's for **cars** / **trains** / **planes**.

2 The Beijing National Stadium:

It's like a bird's **bus** / **nest** / **school**.

It's made of **metal** / **wood** / **glass**.

It has underground **pillars** / **pipes** / **seats**.

## 3 Complete the sentences.

super   metal   airport terminals   Olympics   color

1 Red is the Chinese _____ for good luck.

2 Many buildings were built for the _____ in 2008.

3 Beijing has many _____ structures.

4 Terminal 3 of the Beijing Capital International Airport is one of the biggest _____ _____ .

5 The Beijing National Stadium is one of the biggest _____ buildings.

## 4 Answer the questions.

1 When were the Beijing Olympics?

_____

2 Beijing is the capital of what country?

_____

3 What is the Chinese color for good luck?

_____

4 What is the Beijing National Stadium made of?

_____

5 Write about a sports stadium in your country.

_____

_____

_____

# 6 Different Shapes

← Read pages 14–15.

## 1 Circle the correct words.

The O2:

1 It was built for the **Olympics** / **millennium**.

2 There are 365 **months** / **days** in a year.

3 There are 12 **months** / **days** in a year.

The rotating skyscraper:

4 It can rotate a full **square** / **circle**.

5 It uses energy from the **sun** / **wind**.

6 It can be a different **floor** / **shape** every day.

## 2 Write the months.

September   June   November   February   April   July
~~January~~   December   August   May   March   October

1  January        7  _____

2  _____     8  _____

3  _____     9  _____

4  _____    10  _____

5  _____    11  _____

6  _____    12  _____

## 3 Complete the sentences.

materials  skyscraper  dome
London  day  shapes

1 With new building _____ , people can build structures in different _____ .

2 The O2 is in _____ . It's a _____ .

3 The rotating _____ can change shape every _____ .

## 4 Match. Then write sentences.

The O2

There are 12 months

Every floor can rotate

There are 365 days

The rotating skyscraper uses

in a year.

energy from the wind.

in a year.

is a dome.

a full circle.

1 _The O2 is a dome._

2 _____

3 _____

4 _____

5 _____

# 7 Glass and Ice

← Read pages 16–17.

## 1 Write the words.

> bricks  glass  ice  wood
> concrete  metal  plastic  mud

1 _____

2 _____

3 _____

4 _____

5 _____

6 _____

7 _____

8 _____

## 2 Write *true* or *false*.

1  Ice Hotel is open in January.  _____

2  Ice Hotel is not open in March.  _____

3  Biosphere 2 is a small town.  _____

4  Biosphere 2 is made of glass and wood.  _____

5  There is an ocean in Biosphere 2.  _____

6  There is an ice hotel in Biosphere 2.  _____

## 3 Match.

1 It's made of glass and metal.

2 It's made of ice.

3 It's in Sweden.

4 It's in the USA.

5 It's a research center.

6 I want to go there.

Ice Hotel

Biosphere 2

## 4 Order the words.

1 Ice / Hotel / made / is / ice. / of

   Ice Hotel is made of ice.

2 again. / year / Hotel / is / Every / Ice / built

   _____

3 open / It / from / is / April. / December / to

   _____

4 drinking / glasses / ice. / The / made / of / are

   _____

5 glass / made / Biosphere 2 / of / is / metal. / and

   _____

6 a / is / rainforest / There / in / Biosphere 2.

   _____

# 8 Amazing Places

← Read pages 18–19.

## 1 Match.

1 It's built on ice.
2 It's under the ocean.
3 It moves.
4 It's on skis.

Poseidon
Undersea Resort

Halley 6

## 2 Complete the chart.

~~water~~   cold   skis   submarine   wind
ice   fish   hotel   research   ocean

| Poseidon Undersea Resort | Halley 6 |
|---|---|
| water | _____ |
| _____ | _____ |
| _____ | _____ |
| _____ | _____ |
| _____ | _____ |

### 3 Complete the sentences.

weather   under   on   plastic   moves

1 The Poseidon Undersea Resort is _____ the ocean.

2 The windows are made of a special _____ .

3 Halley 6 is built _____ ice.

4 The ice _____ 400 meters every year.

5 Building in the Antarctic is very difficult because of the _____ .

### 4 Answer the questions.

1 Where is the Poseidon Undersea Resort?

_____

2 Where is Halley 6?

_____

3 How do you get to the Poseidon Undersea Resort?

_____

4 How cold can it be in the Antarctic?

_____

5 What is your favorite structure? Why?

_____

_____

_____

# 9 Structures in Space

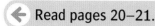 Read pages 20–21.

## 1 Find and write the words.

| a | s | t | r | o | n | a | u | t |
|---|---|---|---|---|---|---|---|---|
| f | r | r | r | t | i | b | p | s |
| a | o | f | e | v | r | i | t | p |
| e | c | u | s | h | h | e | s | a |
| a | k | w | e | s | d | r | o | c |
| r | e | o | a | u | w | r | c | e |
| t | t | o | r | l | i | g | k | c |
| h | e | x | c | n | b | d | c | d |
| b | d | s | h | u | t | t | l | e |

1 a _ _ _ _ _ _ _ _
2 e _ _ _ _ _
3 r _ _ _ _ _ _ _
4 r _ _ _ _ _
5 s _ _ _ _ _ _
6 s _ _ _ _

## 2 Write the numbers.

> 27,700   8   1998   350   16

1 The ISS is _____ kilometers above Earth.

2 It goes around Earth about _____ times every day.

3 It travels at _____ kilometers per hour.

4 It travels at _____ kilometers per second.

5 The first part of the ISS went into space
   in _____ .

## 3 Write the words.

Earth    astronaut    ISS

1 _____     3 _____

2 _____

## 4 Answer the questions.

1 Where is the ISS?

_____

2 What is the ISS?

_____

3 When did the first part of the ISS go into space?

_____

4 How many astronauts went into space with the first part of the ISS?

_____

5 Where do astronauts do spacewalks?

_____

6 Can you see the ISS from Earth?

_____

# 10 Animal Structures

← Read pages 22–23.

**1 Write *true* or *false*.**

1 Termites build their homes with concrete. _____

2 Wombats build burrows underground. _____

3 Wombats bite through things with
their teeth. _____

4 Beavers build dams under the water. _____

5 Beaver dams can be a kilometer long. _____

6 There is a termite mound in my home. _____

**2 Order the words.**

1 too. / Animals / build / can / structures / super

_____

2 mounds / Termite / skyscrapers. / are / termite

_____

3 Wombats / about / meters / dig / hour. / per / 2

_____

4 build / Termites / with / their / mud. / homes

_____

5 dams / Beaver / be / long / a / can / kilometer.

_____

# 3 Complete the puzzle.

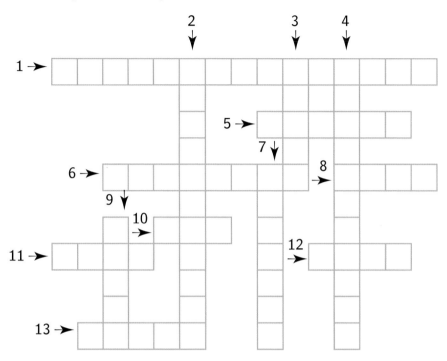

1 It's the name of this book.
2 Very tall buildings are called ___ .
3 An arch dam has a ___ .
4 A tunnel goes here.
5 Beam and suspension are types of ___ .
6 It's a strong building material.
7 Laerdal and Seikan are ___ .
8 In Norway, there is a ___ through a mountain.
9 The Beijing National Stadium is made of ___ .
10 It holds back water.
11 Bridges go ___ water.
12 The Pontchartrain Causeway is very ___ .
13 Biosphere 2 is made of metal and ___ .

# Super Structures in My Country

**1** Complete the chart about super structures in your country.

| What's it called? | What type of structure is it? | How big is it? |
|---|---|---|
|  |  |  |
|  |  |  |
|  |  |  |
|  |  |  |
|  |  |  |
|  |  |  |

**2** Make a poster. Use pictures and write about the super structures.

It's made of …
It's …. meters tall.
It was built in …

**3** Display your poster.

# Design a Super Structure

1 **Think of a super structure.**

2 **Write notes and complete the diagram.**

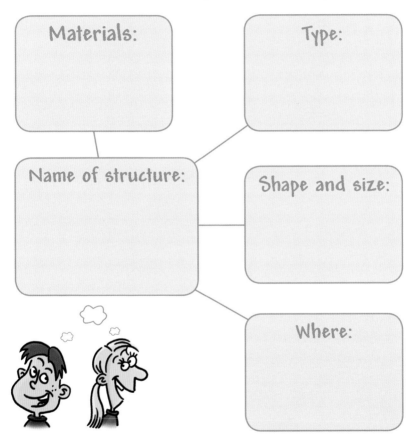

Materials:

Type:

Name of structure:

Shape and size:

Where:

3 **Draw your super structure. Write sentences to describe it.**

4 **Display your design.**

# Picture Dictionary

| bite | bricks | bridge | concrete | dam |

| desert | dig | drinking glass | electricity | flood |

| glass | ground | ice | island | lake |

| metal | million | mine | mountain | mud |